Overgrown

Overgrown

Carolyn Frances Maynard

NEW DEGREE PRESS

OVERGROWN

ISBN   978-1-64137-314-2   *Paperback*
         978-1-64137-608-2   *Ebook*

Contents

Acknowledgements

Even in its simplest, beginning form, this book would not have been possible without some influential individuals. As this book grew, so did the list of people that I owe a debt of gratitude. Firstly, I have to thank my mother and father. Mom, thank you for tempering my doubts and weathering my tirades—thank you for being a steady and loving presence in my life and for fostering strength in me. Dad, thank you for all of the times you shared your uproarious joy with me over my work and successes—thank you for standing by me through difficulty and drama. Abe and Abuelo Papa, thank you for supporting and loving me unconditionally—the work ethic that you both imparted on me is one of the main reasons why this book exists at all.

Thank you to Eric Koester and Brian Bies for making this process manageable and exciting. Also, an especially large thank you to New Degree Press and everyone on my editing and design teams for making my vision into reality.

To Lucas—you suck and you are lucky to be mentioned here at all you little weirdo . . . Obviously kidding, Lucas you have kept me sane for eighteen years and counting. I cannot fully express my gratitude to you without making you uncomfortable with my emotions, so just know that you have inspired me to be myself, in fact to be the best version of myself. You are one of the best people this world has to offer. I am lucky to know you at all, but to call you my brother is one of my life's greatest blessings.

To Danielle and Sana—you are both such captivatingly beautiful souls, and for all intents and purposes you are my sisters. Thank you both for always listening to my nebulous and far-reaching ideas, and grounding me when I venture too far from my path.

To Madison and Tommy, you are both insightful and caring individuals that my life would not be complete without. Thank you for our discussions and shared existential dread. Here's to more adventures and better times ahead.

To Romario, Jess, Jessie, Brittany, and all of my fellow coffee beans . . .

To all of you and many more, thank you—with the whole of my heart.

To you who made me write madly into the next mistakes, you will only last until the end of the page. To you who found me dark and bitter at my first impression, and sweetened me to what you always saw as perfection.

"... I had that familiar conviction that life was beginning over again with the summer."

—F. Scott Fitzgerald, *The Great Gatsby*

Author's Note

To the reader:

Imagine your life as a garden. A space all your own to nourish and grow what you please. What would you grow there? How would you handle the weeds and insects? Would you keep it contained within a picket fence, or let it blossom beyond any confines? This is the essence of the book you are holding.

From the moment you enter our world, navigating life is a beautiful challenge. Growth is a miraculous thing to occur within any of humanity's given circumstances. In a world that is not always kind or supportive, living as a concept can be cyclical and dull, even through our diversity of perspectives. That said, a heart willing to heal and an acknowledgement that suffering is not a requisite of pain can make all the difference in our perception of the world around us, the people in it, and ourselves.

I wrote this book to better foster a connection between my own perspective, emotions, and the world around me. In continuing to grow my collection of poetry for this book, I found that the pieces of my life fit more smoothly together after even a little introspection. This is not a self-help book, nor is it a cautionary tale. In fact, it was hardly supposed to be a book in the first place. This collection is an anthology of living through a single lens. The only thing that has remained consistent throughout my experiences, that I hope comes across clearly in my work, is a sense of gratitude and purpose.

....

I have been drawn to floral and natural imagery in my writing for as long as I can remember. The ease and applicability of a comparison between personal growth and the cycle of life, death, and rebirth in nature has made a lot of challenges in my life much more bearable. You will notice an abundance of the poems in this book are titled with names of flowers. This is more than a nod to the aforementioned cycle of life; it is also a celebration of the diversity, color, and absolute beauty that the world has to offer.

Although an element of nature will appear in almost every piece, this book is not just a cursory look at our world through the lens of our natural environment. My work is an attempt to capture the intricacies of life, death, and rebirth as seen through a variety of my life experiences. In their simplest form, these concepts may appear mundane and elicit cynicism, but each poem in this book is a piece of a larger whole—each a desire to escape that cynicism and keep wonder for every facet of life.

I was born in the month of **August**, so naturally it is the first chapter. As such, the poems within that section have to do with emerging into awareness and an excitement for being alive. Due to a serious heart condition, there have been several moments where in my life I thought I would not make it. Therefore, I have grown up believing that every moment we *are* alive should be a celebration of the chances we are all given every day. All of my pieces are open to interpretation at the reader's discretion, but I hope that these elements come through, as I am a firm believer in making the most out of what you have.

Next is **October**. These poems are an autumnal, somber reflection on universal difficulties that people face, as well as some specific difficulties I have experienced. Heart-breaks, changing relationship dynamics, and a disdain for people who intentionally do harm are all subjects in this section. This chapter addresses topics that mirror attributes of the fall season, but it is called October for my associations of the aforementioned topics with this month specifically.

November is comprised of a variety of softer and some darker pieces. Fueled by nostalgia, despondence, and a harsher season, this chapter is overall an attempt to cling to the past either through anger or better memories. However, the culmination of this chapter is a release of the fleeting or already gone in favor of new beginnings.

April is the heart of the spring season — completely decorated with life that isn't necessarily new, just reborn into a new time. Many of the pieces in this chapter are love poems, though some may not appear that way. This section is celebratory and reverential of the people and emotions that make life worth living, regardless of the length of time they are with us or their imperfections. This is the book's second beginning, and it will not be its last.

I am incredibly happy to be able to publish this collection after loving poetry and writing for most of my life. As I write this—in August, 2019—I am content with a sense of coming full circle. I have experienced losses and beautiful beginnings, usually becoming aware of them only after they have occurred. Just as I have come full circle with this collection, I am ready to go around again to see what more I can create and enjoy from this life.

Living means change—growth. People will come and go, relationships will deteriorate or flourish in ways you could never expect, but it is all worth it. Keep a wonder for the world and your own place in it, for the dynamic moments that define us and those that go unnoticed. Thank you so much for reading, I hope you enjoy the book.

—Carolyn

August

Perennial

Born in broken gold,
Laying bare with the flowers,
Rooted in the fertile ground,
Freckled with crumbling ruins,
Breathing simply strong and free
In these timeless, passing days,
Watching, passive in the mornings'
Foggy heaven, a rising dewdrop haze.

Divine shimmer of the infinite
Stars fading into age and ashes,
I am entrenched in the earth,
Metallic eyes seasoned with rust,
As the eternal turns fossil, and
The sky has lost its blue,
Wandering through this body of scars,
I'm an open wound.

Thoughts for the Ocean

The lifted bird is effervescent,
Shining as she sings freedom
To a covered, cloudy horizon

Nested, that thunder
Had clipped her wings,
And the earth became
Her cage in storm

Rain falls unnoticed to the ocean,
Unbothered, the fish swims
With deliberation in peaceful tune

The fish could desire the bird
To drown for his perspective,
Just as she could have him
Flounder at the depth he
Perceives a surface

The difference lies not within
The eyes of God and comprehension,
Our shades of sky and ocean lie
In the beliefs of our suspension.

Buried

Black pearl,   White pearl

rich and full,   silken shell

raw and only,   commonly lonely

tough and comely,   suited and strung

of ocean's grandeur   like grains of sand

Whales and Foxes

welcome to the world
where perfection lies
scattered in the few
moments of content,

where the infant prose
you're told are lessons
lost on those too old,

and the love you tell
me I will one day find,
I reserve in awe
for those of your kind

Lucas

Relentless, a heart willing to forgive finds few mercies
Time will not return and smile for the wonder in your
mind
Do not fall to your knees against their concrete will,
And lament the bruises on your skin to shroud yourself
within

....

You are the undoubted sunrise over the plain
That only glows for glory own, but never grows in vain
Turned to quiet fire, sparked alone—let it be
Let it be a peaceful light, in practice and in name.

Childish

I flew before you left the rye,
and fire claims quickly
any left behind

I landed, burning remorse
soot-stained, battered,
purging our perversions

I looked for you in my arms,
but you were rooted
at my side

You rose like embers to heaven,
smiling that we had won,
steadied by the sun.

in the quiet hours

in the quiet hours
i muse with joy,
and it has your face

i dream the words
i'll write and sing
i dream of painting
with the colors
behind my eyes

i remember every time
you brought me a smile,
and mine is fresh, ripened
with memory—sweetened
to perfection

hearing again what we said,
so i can listen, drawing
pictures in my head
to paper the walls of my mind

my favorite is the street side
yellow sky reflected in mine –
the way you step into the world

my favorite is there again,
before the bitter winds had
summer surrender to its doubt

my favorites are the kindred

souls that cross to my path
and find some purpose here

these are my tapestry,
a great mural of all
that is good

in the quiet hours,
i take actualizing form,
but through the braving
past the walls,
this tapestry is worn

Awakening

Saccharine chords of memory
Sapling dripping dew and dawn
In the morning of grief grown old
We begin new lifetimes
Already told.

Rose Garden

Of all the red blooms in the garden
Singled out and plucked gently,
This is the most saccharine rose

Freshly strewn in perfect disarray
Wine colored in candle light and
Pressed until the petals smell like sweat

You waited and held fast with torn
Heart and photographs as they wilted,
Long past the stench of certain death

Green - veined stem, thick with thorns,
Draws dark ochre from your fingertips
Red like you, she hates this part of her

Paraded and ripped from home
Surrendering earth's aroma to the air
Known only to her - her sweet sepulcher

How do you come back from roses?
Live only in memory?
A hedonistic haze.

Faith

I have built my own casket, and dug my own grave
I have filled the ground with thornless white roses,
And I sit atop my headstone, carving in my name,
Watching the sun rise, set, then fade
Back to the star born from heaven's hearth
Away, away from me and my frost - laced eyes,
In crystalline solitude, I watch the empty sky,
And this is what I call faith.

Ending, Ill-Advised

Rain the thoughts of Rome,
Cluttered in the air, sharp as clouds
Whose arms reach from me to here

To ripple all the pooled perfection,
To wish a return by the fountain,
To venture there at all,

Crumbling like a conquered city, fading
On a summer breeze—compared as
Apples to oranges, or ashes to dust

I can only let the breeze breathe for me,
And carry me toward what empire awaits

Bright Eyes

New life, she dances and sings every time
Ancient mind, older soul, fire burning
With darkening coal—bright ember eyes
She performs wild—imagine fields
Of lightning and undying flowers
She is the sun, bathed in rain showers

Do not inherit hurt from the weak
Who ask for love but do not bother to seek
Beauty and the worth of joy alone
Only worn from weather, and whether
The day will come again

She'll lie loose in her tulle and lace
Long with the hours passing over golden
Earth—wind dances carry her home
We master the burden and hold the world
On soft shoulders and strong smiles,
Parting to cast love in the decaying air

Cries to a heart that shares her ache
Not of pity or fear, but silencing light,
Thinning breath to air out stale murmurs
Powerful, but too strong—often
Does she see a wash of cloudy gaze,
Gray as storm in fair weather

Perennial soul—fighting, peaceful arms
Bearing only the connection to the chest
And telling you what her heart shouts to nothing

Moving in a forest of burning, bodiless voices
What pause does she make, to extend her hand?
Hopeful meeting - I see you, bright eyes.

Retrospect

You cannot have me to hold,
Waving a flag of conquest
Over open earth for redress
Of your burdens and explored
In awe, uncertain and enraptured

You flowed like a halo and cut
My sharpened stare, curling breeze
Over land laid bare —
You could not bear
To leave

Should you venture on,
Or run frightened to the hills,
Mind the soil caked in your boots,
The grass in your hair,
The ache in your muscles,
And the living breath
Lifted in your chest

Tired, you confess a need,
And settle in the ground,
Mind the lips that kissed
Mine, letting truth subside,
Are those uttering your vows.

Fearless Woman

Tell me
I am not afraid
To be the woman—she who stands
Whole and unburdened toward the waves
Of doubt that wash the minds of fellows,
And shift the monuments as dust

I do not stand alone
My sister breathes in measure,
My brother holds my heart together
Untaken by a weightless, iron will
To move with the tides, but not
Bend for rain and simple storm

We see the salt in the water
As it stings our open eyes,
And runs throughout our bodies
In the blood of examined lives

All with no exceptions—mustering
Choked out words at refused silence,
Creating, when meaning turns mundane,
Deaf only to sirens of security,
And the carelessness of ease

Beyond discrepancies and disagreement,
Below the surface, we know our common
Colors of desire and need—shared face
To swim the waters of our past with dignity
And humbly reach harmony and peaceful shores

The fearless people do not ignore
Salt in their wounds, saturated in the seas
Born reeling with jagged scars
We do not deny what is
Given and born coursing through us
Like a current, in our veins,
But with no hesitance we will defy
To drown in ignorance or in pain.

For August

miracle is her soft surrender
to the warm colors of the cold,
her resilience for the broken hearts,
and patience with their heresies told
returning life through time and again,
for the immutable will that cannot bend,
August is neither her beginning nor end.

October

epitaph

mourning in the graveyard,
dawn breaks over what is best
kept in the dark, strong - willed and
persistent, the sun rises all too distant,
casting shadows from the stones
that penetrate the infertile ground.

dewdrop tears rain upwards
from the earth, and rise calmly
to softly shroud any blossoms
that dare to bloom in the rot.

shuffling alone between memories,
deeper down their path—bold
enough to escape the light,
stumbling over broken stones, until
an aching washes away the doubt.

pushed forth from the cold, consuming
taunting shadows, granted a thin halo
from the light in which you lie,
they're empty and waiting—void of hope,
no disappointment, no wonder.

glance back as dusk falls over
what you blissfully forgot –
consider at last the ruins,
of the monuments gone wrong
while ghosts stand in the mirror
watching.

Silent Refrain

kept too long, the child mind
will grow in disappointment,
at how the soulful notion
they held so high in hope,
and higher in regard is

often held in secret, and
in secret - not at all,
that sung unknown to
the subjects of our suffered
silences and pleas to God
is the heart's daily refrain,

that our captivated souls
will worship in hope of release,
and those foolish enough
to betray the lock and key
will find it creates nothing —
no miracle, but misery.

I Stopped Listening

Many know the first island found adrift at sea,
its corruptions clear to the eye looking back,
its intoxicating paradise glaring through the pupils.

In my eyes, a crystal glaze, glossing what
could not pierce my gaze as I slipped
on my best dress and widest smile,
tripping over the minutes with you,
that littered my days like boulders in the sand.

Walking miles on shifting sands
toward you, weaving your web below,
I felt the plunge only too late,
and fell right through –
certain only in certain fate.

Abandoned to the vastness, I opened my eyes
to see the sky that had not changed,
even while I had looked away,
thinking that the stars
resided in my eyes.

Profoundly introduced, I do not miss
the wild springs and dancing fountains of those
hollowed paradisal grounds.

I relinquish and forgive someone else's foreign shore.

Subtlety

If shamelessly, the vulture flies
And you have no contrition for cries
Then why should I apologize
For my lack of subtlety?

That man left the light off,
I'm deep purple like a bruise,
Puerile boy –
You may call me Violet Woman.

Persistent, singular
Not another weak in sequence
To satiate you, or wake
With you.

You've a talent to violate from within.

You are worth neither hatred nor reprieve
Yet asking for both, you'll run away
And wonder what is left of me.

Nothing you knew,
What was delicate like faith,
I ripped wildly beyond recall,
And the rest lays screaming,
(in the woods by the water tower)
Convincing the rain to stay.

The memories I cannot hide
Between my locked legs reside,

Because you knew
I was not ready,
And not in touching nor in fleeing,

Did you have any sense of subtlety.

Yellow River

An afternoon to wonder through clouds,
how long she has been running,
lifting water over falls,
and carrying life between the rocks.

My yellow toes, eager to feel
DO
her cool touch, recoil and send
NOT SWIM
pulses of nausea to my stomach.
IN THE RIVER

Up and over the edge,
up to the granite shore
lay a noxious decay
poisoned at the depths
that venom could never reach,

A toxic disturbance,
forced upon her
as her prayers and howls
alike drowned before her
in the runoff, overflowed.

Longing to run wild and be known,
but late in her futility, she works and lies,
waiting for the world to lift her veil,
to be found - reprieved - to be seen

I'll sit and wind through thoughts with her,

waiting for the yellow sun to sit and start anew
my blood runs like her, in circles around
my heart thinking how to sift through,
to share only purity and gold.

Resonance

Wounded by scathing impatience
Like a broken phonograph,
Or one doomed to hear it
on repeat
repeat

How can the deaf man
hear his own remorse?
How can the blind man
see his faults with clarity?

In the way that you perceive
Consequences void of reason
Fueling your damned lament

I have shattered my glass cage,
And your desperate, raging breath
Makes yours opaque along the fault lines

The muted rings of melancholy
Echo pleasantly between the shards
A softer tone to beg and remind
My ire cannot leave you behind.

Wakeful and The Watchman

Unlit room of velvet, loose with fear
Name not resting long on our lips
Felt through the cracks in the floor,
And in sweeping, dreadful silence.

He is watching.

Musings reach the crumbling walls
For purpose, moving past a poor facade
With a mind that solace won't come back for,
Held by the sacred that had escaped.

Sheltered

faded memories of innocence
a house timed by mold and dust
playing at infancy for too long
family retriever—golden boy
every man a grand saint and hero
in the eyes of children, but too
often did he bare his teeth,
and snarl at small ones
scratching at the confused, joyful hearts

old dog, left brutal and disturbed
with age and irritation, clinging
to the knees of growing children,
bringing them crashing down

these children, born to him saviors
and older now, he is just
a nuisance, whining, crying
that no one would attend
his fragile will and false amend

some obligation has them—grown,
working, living, and torn
to the homes they made away
from the hurt and poisoned house
they cannot carry him like
a child, helpless to their mercy—gone
with no breath for crying at scars

Arson

The arsonist carries with him a flame,
Thinking the smoke is not his fault
How could we burn within a shroud?
Where is the proof among our ashes?
Entity of anguish, purposeless in practice
Burning each edifice like a work of art

Broken harmony with the air,
Our breath and burning sun,
Always running away, as if strangely unaware
Of what he's done for a forgotten time

He never stays to watch the burn –
When and should the arsonist return,
His eyes will be glazed with memory
Believing all the emptiness he sees
A canvas, woven soft and suited to him
In his ignorance

He never sees the phoenix, strong
To rise again, to be wise again
She knows the arsonist is blind, so
Solace only in her tearshed does she find.

Fearful Man

Witness the mundane as man –
Swilling whiskey and vapor,
Sitting at a table with no legs,
Waging war with his enemies
Waging war with his friends

He drones with the rain,
And perceives his words
Thunder—boasting:
A man is tedious without fear

Within the room of averted gaze,
Lulled by the froth of his mind,
To the fearful, against
Repetition and refrain,
He'll nod his head, and
Raise his glass

They would not
Grace his table;
Their fear is
An impassioned flight,
And his is volume for substance,
An unnamed submission,
As a torch to sunlight

Wither

The dandelions that never fly,
and the unpicked rose's lament
Shriveling from their stems too high,
Refusing life for detriment

Wither those that stay?
Like shadows, blooming
In unnoticed rapture
As their petals fall away

Do we call their death a silence,
If they cannot cry to hear?
No butterfly nor hummingbird
Does a wilting flower fear

Revisiting Pearls

Choke me with a string of pearls,
That cascades over me to the ground
Until the thread breaks and they
Scatter—not again to be found

From my bed, I'll wade the white
Beads of bashful, pathetic conception
A pearl knows how a ray throws light,
Sun against the moon — a dull reflection

Opaque, each with something to hide,
Luxurious together, but ridiculous and plain
Containing the same mystery inside,
Yet each concealed thinly and in vain

Watch for my heel, your shell will dust
Crushing pearls for conquer and lust

Dripping crystals and silks
I'll stay awake on velvet concrete
One hand ready for a single call,
Not waiting to slip on another and fall

I'll make myself a diamond,
Cutting, clear and devastating
Refined and absolute,
Granted color by the sky,
And glowing from her hue.

Cracks in Stained Glass

The fear you give me
Unknowingly, stays
Rested in my veins

Not for a sense of danger,
Not for another risk of pain

I fear myself a barricaded door,
Ready to be opened,
Or a stained glass window
Watching a smirking child,
With pebbles in his hands

I am afraid of you,
Because your hands
Redressed me in conviction,
And tore my breath from me

Whirlwind

No journey is ended in absence
Footprints lose their form to futility,
Knowing they have been made,
And all our buried pen strokes
Riot to be saved

I have run, exhausted and afraid,
I have run, and called it travel,
I have toiled for simple glories,
To piece the world together,
And hope to change

Only to find that bricks are bricks
On either side of the walls,
Crashed through by forlorn horses,
Bolting from their saddles, and deaf
To desperate calls

So for the walls I have helped to build,
I will never meet you again, but maybe
If you trace your finger on the cracks —
Take care, for no reigns can hold me back,
Or lessen my impact.

Held in the Sky

I remember. Dancing with you,
Twisting in your sixties' kitchen
My brother laughs, stop and go,
Held in your heart and your eyes
Childhood was your effortless disguise.

Woman for her name alone held more
Than motherhood and strength could know
Dancing in their dreams, a legacy fabricated
In memory

How could we look through her?
I see mine through your life,
And hope to sing her sacrifices
As yours and a gift of mine

That we may live more easily
That we may live at all
While you remain our atlas
And we have yet to crawl.

November

Fig Tree

Bourbon blossoms through the smoke
Winding through foggy remembrance,
And parting with the air to return to winter

I am lost to seasons over my shoulder,
As I peek behind, not seeking nor hoping to find
There are the running children, climbing fences,
And plucking from the fig tree until a haze sets again

If I walk and close my eyes to the bricks and crystal
walls
My baby, she's in burgundy. My baby she's in
kelly green.
They're walking, running—they laugh like they've
never seen
My face before, and here it is again –
Familiar like a star that shines brightest now and then

If I go, will they run back to me?
If I go, will I come back?
If I go, they will run to me

The season turning around me is counterfeit and silent
The leaves drop without a whisper, they say enough –
On the branch, backing away, I am last and left to fall.

Junkie

She lies lethargic, cushioned between her lungs
Desperate and despondent The weight is crushing
She scratches at her arms, get out, get off
Hit, just one more hit
Another
Now. Please.

Pick it up—no, damn it—put it down.
Have some damn pride—cling
To threads Any remaining shreds of
self-respect slowly
Time passes with its own pace

She lies, looking at her life
– the longest sentence
Her eyes, like the ticking clock, twitch and stop.
Among old highs and her comfortable low
She beats fast, thrust forward then –

Pulse! broken beats throb and cry
Familiar movement in fragile fingers
Worst when it doesn't work, nothing happens
But wait, the tingling—ecstasy in anticipation

the adrenaline washes the guilt clean like gold paint

She lies to everyone, letting no clue slip,
An expert in her art, she breathes heavy again,
The high goes down, she rests and beats slow
This is it for me, she says, until
it all runs out.

Unassuming

Silent shoes whisper to the ground
Everyday jeans and a nondescript blouse,
blue, and blushing sickly orange,
small like a fawn—the song in my ears

Just enough makeup so you can tell
she's there—to fill in the sleepless circles
Figure of very little consequence,
a pretty, kind of cloudy day face

Hands with old, soft calluses, only
just big enough, strong enough
to catch and hold the rain
until they are told at last to let go
They hoist up the black, monolithic
bag on their shoulders, and it is
twice the size of this fragile form

Reflecting inside, the coming storm

Noise

You are relentless.
There is absolutely no escape
From your presence
Searching for a small haven
Where only God will listen,
I ask you why –

Why are you this way?
How can you apologize
Through eyes that see no fault?
How can you say you love me
With a mouth full of disgust?

How dare you say you understand
When you are Narcissus, and
I am the futile pond?
How can you listen to me,
When you only hear yourself?

Go away, damn you,
I am not your object of reflection,
I am not your tool
I am not your shiny toy –
To break and fix as you please

I hate how I catch myself
Thinking the way you do
I hate how you walk away,
And come back as if you never left.

All seduced
By simple fixes,
And slammed doors –
Satisfaction never for a
Change of heart

Spitting rage at your ignorance,
When mine is plain to see
I want to believe we can
Keep this a secret—
Let it be unspoken
That those who really matter
Look past hypocrisy

Thoughts for the Fish Bowl

floating.
pushed away in waves, drifting
driven toward something,
unknown, nothing
accompanied from the distance,
by fellow lost and tired souls
some take my hand
some squeeze it, fuse with it
those who cast their hearts away
scorn us from the shore
let them spin their heads,
until they fall off
they have no idea,
comfortable in their calluses,
asking why we bleed when they strike,
strangling while telling us to breathe
they have no idea
how to live estranged from death
bringing themselves to the edge –
it's the answer to every simple trial
I have no edge; the ocean will swallow me,
bind my legs so I cannot tread
it's not up to me,
but I am emboldened by the certainty
I lived on the sands of mortality,
an island where I keep my pen and paint
appealing ocean, I dove in—too fast,
the current pulled me back to drown
I'm done gasping, quenched by salt water,
they keep the ropes close to their chests,

and feign it round their necks
mouth breathing spinning heads
and anger crashes into me
like a breaking wave
against the sand
float with me,
I'll appreciate the company.

Georgia Will Be Here

were you going to tell me
that I was going to lose you?
did I even come to mind?
your whirlwind and circumstance
already left me behind.

....

to be more than a string,
or a whisper on the breeze
I can see through
a distance and
a silence.

....

you know me like
a city knows its stars,
and you come back flying
like constellations,
claiming that the sky
has shifted.

Barren

Today, God has forgotten to paint the sky,
and I have forgotten to smile at the blue and yellow
For before my eyes lies a muted red
all but enraged at the spectacle of dust,
I hold the void in my hands,
and it feels like it's mine.

Please Find Sun

You imagine a mirrored facade,
And what must it show the world
As we are supposedly so alike –
Supposed to be

You could be arbitrary,
You could be perfect,
You could stay with me,
In step with our labored breaths

We were seamless like the sea,
On which you let me drift,
Never missing an anchor,
So just as often will I feel
Your absence in every dawn.

Hourglass Phoenix

Knock me down now
While I may still get up
Without wasting a moment,
Still infatuated and high

Burn me now till I blaze
My ashen dress will dust away
To reveal smooth skin and ember eyes

Lie through your teeth
Before words have meaning
Or else they never will

Hurt me while there's still hope
For me to push back with a smile
And raised brow, curving for your desire

Love me when my heels are too high,
Love me when my head is too heavy,
When sugar becomes bitter crystals,
And the cries are beyond strength and control

Now do your worst,
Until my wings are unmet with mercy
Plummeting beside me—silently,
Gracefully

Fixed with Gold

Laced with cracks
A vase of daisies
Lies waiting to be

Dropped and fallen,
Until gone and forgotten,
It prays to shatter
Beyond repair

That the broken glass may shatter,
That the grains of sand will crack,
That the atoms will rupture,
Until it breathes singular and still

So light may catch it
After meeting the ground,
And marvel in its tragic beauty

Reset

There is nothing left, but
Walls stripped white
A clock that turns back
In agony, around an empty face

Inward to infinite, inviting
Archways to unmade memories
Thrust out again to fits of rage
Against a soft horizon

Tell me I never loved,
And I'll believe it
In an instant
Desperately

Rumor

Two photographs
A handful of songs
Hair like yours, shortened
An epigraph too long

Do you feel the held
Hands, like held breath
Waiting in vain—a heart kept
In the dark on a silver chain

You've left flickering embers
In your wake, reignited
Only for our selfish sake

Memories rot like rumors
Until uncertain, our bodies freeze,
But I can feel you dancing too —
Our music brings the earth to me

A gentle chord drawn out to grieve,
My longing child begs your reprieve.

Absolve

heal the mother
who watches her son,
choking on the dust of comets
fallen harshly to the earth
forgotten by the watchers
since their race across the sky

she gave life to her heaven,
and bore the earth to him,
limited by the reach of her arms
and brokenhearted
by his strained chords,
ripping at his roots

rageless, she prays
in burning churches,
by muddy rivers,
as he becomes so
beyond her reach
that he must be golden

Pebbles

Halt the ticking clock of yours,
And cast the pearls outside,

That they may be seeds of wonder
Growing from a lack of time.

Pave your paces forward if given
Nothing but fear and fruitless ambition,

But pause to wish on every dandelion
That persists between the cracks.

Come Back With the Saints

Alone between pews
as blades of grass,
back to the sinners,
that worship as they're born

Guilt in one hand,
Pride in the other
Eyes distracted,
North star heart

Now unsure, maybe
That the path lies ahead
Less painful, or perhaps
It will circle around again

Come back with the saints,
Or in winter, burning towards me
I'll be in danger
To never doubt again.

April

Interlude

I woke up dressed in sun,
Fallen from the midnight sky,
The stars winked that I had
Been there before

I stared down,
I looked up,
And each moment was
So familiar

Contemplating my rippled face,
That was yours at our meeting place

As the crystals shed their tears,
And the stardust loosed its fears
You spelled glory on my lips,
And stopped to keep me here

The rest are all for you,
That carry notes of sweetness,
And every hopeful breath
Always held your name

Singing for our interlude,
Wishing for our reprieve,
Waiting –

To be
Yours,

Deeply, fully, unapologetically –

I love you

Sunflower

Here I am with mortal eyes,
professing my love for you

On the eroding ruins,
past my futile footprints

Too, I make known all
the loveliest labors

Made facing loss and
soon buried, gone in rot

Star-crossed like sunflowers
turning away from the sun

This love will last even
if not with me—it will

Run on, like the never
still name of rain

But here, I root my landslide self
into the ignorant, corrosive ground.

Charming

You hit my eyes
like stars on still water,
reflective, then deeply fallen.
You ripple me to a glistening obscurity.
You are the sun and horizon
after our nights alone,
I radiate with you.

Serendipity

Deafening only to my own intuition,
My spirit is loud with life like you
Wide as the sun and twice as bright.

Only barely spoken from behind
How I see your glow — in the tumult
and rain, souls back to that refrain
Of this ecstatic pulse, it doesn't tire,

It doesn't wake for it stays dreaming
Wishing it is real, widening electric eyes
To fill those pools with reflections of
Rippling water, flirting with overflow

Surrender

Suddenly short and small and shallow –unfound,
Like a pond about to lose herself to the ocean
I spiral in my own current as I stand aside and watch
My heart fail again—I am on that same precipice,
Dreading the drop, but already having taken the fall.

My waters are stale from running too long and hard
Through unhallowed ground under fogs of
Fear and needed doubt
That clouded my sun
For too long.

One voice says speak, the other dares to die
Rather than look up, look them in the eye
Commanding surrender, certain to
Break your dream gaze,
Slowly, then your heart.

I have so much to say to the world beyond them,
But I've kept that name in my mouth for so long,
That it too has grown stale—withheld breath
Pales my face over and over
Almost over.

Held Breath

This hope is trusting
as the first breath in waking,
but dangerous as the last before sleep

That we can weave between possibility
and futility, to survive long enough
to draw breath together,
and let hope rest.

Haven

Hills for relinquish,
paths of running ants,
and wild berries in summer

A springtime lullaby for
Forsaken wandering
through air lost in words

Love this place,
for its green grass
and magnetic waterfalls

But secretly it smiles,
knowing what was
surrendered to the skies

A powerless prayer,
Miraculous cries,
and a return to grace

So too, must you see
This place as a haven

every time

you paint for me a gilded picture of golden promise,
I am unsure if you comprehend its beauty,
lightened until it pales to yours,

but true to the words of the immortal king
beautiful one, you always shatter
the pictures, like the mirror in your mind
every time

Hyacinth Girl

Cruel and darling April,
that in it I should fall in love
with the blooming flowers
the rich and gentle woods,

With a single gaze at what
is within the Earth
and the whispered tones
of a true bird's song,

Only to feel the breath
of life on my neck and shoulder
and my ember heart turn to ash,
after April promised to last.

Sober

Darling, you break my heart
Every day
You know that?
Yes, I told you
(What can words do better than walking away?)
Sorry
It's hardly any fault of yours
Keeping closed with practiced words,
My heart simply loves
To break

She lets her words fall
Out and run through me
She says to me,

Look at that
Look at what could be—beautiful

With her I can practically see
What practically will never be
My heart simply loves
To break
In saying you are
Everything,
Knowing
Everything's at stake

Hummingbird

Wake to a broken beat,
As a hummingbird flight
With clipped wings

Yellow inside, bruised with nectar
Buttercups for violets, waiting
To grow with drowsy breaths

To fill the time we left behind
With our heartstrings playing
A wintery, safe refrain

Revisiting Sunflowers

That we were just sunflowers, growing side by side,
Bearing no thorns, rearing heads born toward the sky.
As time circles us—its prey, I catch your fallen petals,
Though planted in my memory they soon dissolve
to dirt.

That we were just simple flowers, and not souls bound
to mind,
Carefully the sound of whispers of more than the held
breath
Of sacred friendship that only few will find.

Synergy

captured in pulses,
you are unavoidable
in memory, a permanence
elusive, never again to be held

painting you to reality,
the colors never mix properly
always a shade off —

the black of my shoes is scuffed
the red in your hair is all I remember
and there is no glow against your cheek
coming from behind the door

you're a portrait of answered prayers
hung in hallways before the rain
and when you pass on the concrete,
I become a statue, as the frame breaks away

Conditional

If we are caught
As raindrops dancing
Between blades,
Entropic for sleepless
Nights—dragged through
Brazen daylight, pulling away,

I will soak in the earth,
Rich and corrupted until
Your call, and with rise
And fall, we'll be drifting
In between the dawns,
Singing like new canaries,

And born to the laughter
Of life becoming—we are
Held, enraptured and apart
Until our infant babbles tell
Him at the hopeful ascent
How it feels—
Like heaven.

Wisteria

The wisteria bloomed again,
At long last without finality,
And there I was at the fence
Saturated with delight,
Vibrant like a new film

Like the one I was promised
Without an oath,
And never saw.

There we were, fast and flawless
Like a minute between moments

....

I felt the fresh swells of purple
Turned from light to lavender,
And I bore my soul behind the garden wall,
Her pansies in my hair –

Behind my gilded fence did fall
Drops of amber and sighs of pleasure
As the suns and moons danced together
For a rippled instant, I wove between
The mirror's sweetness and the shards
Opening the gates, stepping to my petal pace

The wild flowers paint me
In painless purple before unknown
Lasting until the wisteria must go home,

For the scattered seconds I am not alone,
I am beautifully overgrown.

www.ingramcontent.com/pod-product-compliance
Lightning Source LLC
Chambersburg PA
CBHW071525180526
45171CB00002B/380